LEGACY BY DESIGN

A 12-Week Journey to Reclaim Your Identity, Set Boundaries, and Build a Sustainable Life & Legacy

HealingWorks® | Anastacia Sams, MA, LMFT, Founder & CEO

Copyright © 2026 HealingWorks®, LLC
All rights reserved.

No part of this publication may be reproduced, distributed, stored, or transmitted in any form or by any means, electronic or mechanical, including photocopying, recording, or other information storage and retrieval systems, without the prior written permission of the publisher, except in the case of brief quotations embodied in critical reviews or articles.

Legacy by Design™: A 12-Week Guided Workbook is a proprietary book and an integral component of the **HealingWorks® Legacy Framework™**, a protected methodology developed by HealingWorks®, LLC. All concepts, language, exercises, and frameworks in this work are the exclusive intellectual property of HealingWorks®, LLC.

ISBN-13: 979-8-218-93313-5

First Edition, 2026

Published by:
HealingWorks®, LLC
7535 E. Hampden Ave, Suite 400, Denver, CO 80231

Published in the United States of America

Publisher Website:
www.healingworks.co

This workbook is intended for educational and reflective purposes only. It is not a replacement for therapy, counseling, medical care, or professional mental health services. Readers are encouraged to seek appropriate professional support as needed.

HealingWorks® and HealingWorks® Legacy Framework™ are trademarks and/or service marks of HealingWorks®, PLLC.

Printed in the United States of America.

TABLE OF CONTENTS

Introduction
Before You Begin
How to Use This Workbook
Author's Note

Week 1 — Mapping Your Life Story

Identity, Culture & Origin Patterns

Week 2 — Intergenerational Mapping

Emotional Inheritance, Patterns & Survival Roles

Week 3 — Unlearning Survival Scripts

Internal Boundaries, Deconditioning & Identity Reclamation

Week 4 — Returning to Values

Values-Based Living, Identity Integration & Direction

Week 5 — Body Awareness & Nervous System Literacy

Listening to Internal Signals

Week 6 — Energy Boundaries & Capacity Protection

Stewarding Your Energy

Week 7 — Returning to the Self

Reclaiming the Parts You Silenced

Week 8 — Rituals, Rhythms & Sustainability

Consistency That Holds What Matters

Week 9 — Values-Based Decision Making & Self-Trust

Choosing from Internal Direction

Week 10 — Purpose, Vision & Legacy Orientation

Designing the Life You Are Meant to Live

Week 11 — The Five Pillars of a Sovereign Life

Creating a Foundation That Holds What You Build

Week 12 — The Legacy Manifesto & Sustainability Plan

Living What You've Clarified

Closing Note

Living Your Legacy

BEFORE YOU BEGIN

This workbook is created as a guide for reflection, healing, and alignment. It is not a replacement for therapy, counseling, or medical care. Please seek professional support if needed. All content is original work and may not be reproduced, distributed, or adapted without written permission from HealingWorks®.

HOW TO USE THIS WORKBOOK

A Guide for a 12-Week Return to Self

This workbook is designed to be experienced slowly, and intentionally, over twelve weeks. Each week builds on the last, not by adding pressure, but by deepening integration. The pacing matters. It allows insight to settle into the body, values to move into behavior, and reflection to become lived alignment.

You are not meant to complete this perfectly. You are meant to complete it honestly. Some weeks may move you quickly; others may ask you to linger. If something stirs emotion, resistance, or fatigue, that is information you can use on this journey. Pause when needed. Return when you're ready.

You may find it helpful to choose a consistent rhythm for your work (the same day or time each week), but flexibility is welcome. This workbook is not linear in the way productivity tools are; it is cyclical. You will revisit themes—identity, boundaries, values, rest—from new vantage points as you evolve.

Integration is happening when you notice small but meaningful shifts: clearer decision-making, reduced urgency, increased self-trust, or a deeper sense of internal coherence.

Lastly, at the end of each week is a notes section for you to journal your reflections and insights.

AUTHOR'S NOTE

A Grounded Word Before You Begin

This workbook is shaped by more than a decade of my clinical work as a licensed marriage and family therapist, leadership development, and close witnessing of how high-capacity people learn to survive—often at the expense of themselves. It is also shaped by cultural memory, relational wisdom, and the truth that healing does not happen through insight alone, but through integration and aligned action.

You will not find quick fixes here. What you will find is structure, language, and reflection designed to help you tell the truth to yourself—gently, clearly, and without self-abandonment. Every exercise is an invitation into right relationship with yourself.

This work honors both where you come from and where you are going. It respects your resilience while making room for rest. My hope is that as you move through these pages, you feel supported, and that you experience yourself as capable of leading your life from within.

WELCOME

You are stepping into a journey of remembering, releasing, and rebuilding.

This workbook is not about becoming someone new — it's about returning to yourself, i.e. who you are beneath the expectations, the roles, the survival patterns, and the pressure to perform. Over the next twelve weeks, you'll explore the stories that shaped you, the patterns you inherited, the beliefs you've outgrown, and the values that anchor who you are becoming.

Take your time. Some weeks will feel tender. Some will feel liberating. All of them are opportunities to reclaim your energy, your voice, your truth, and your direction.

This is not a race. It's a return.
A return to alignment.
A return to wholeness.
A return to the life you are meant to lead.

Welcome home to yourself.

WEEK 1: Mapping Your Life Story

Every life is shaped by story. Long before you consciously chose who to become, *you were absorbing messages about who you needed to be.* Family dynamics, cultural expectations, educational environments, and social conditions all contributed to how you learned to move through the world.

This week centers on understanding identity as something shaped through experience. The beliefs you hold about success, worth, responsibility, and strength did not emerge in isolation. They were formed through moments, environments, and relationships that taught you what was rewarded, what was discouraged, and what felt necessary for survival.

Many people carry inherited narratives without realizing it. These narratives influence ambition, self-expectation, and how pressure is interpreted. They also shape how rest, emotion, and self-expression are experienced. Mapping your life story brings these influences into view.

This work invites you to trace formative moments that shaped your understanding of who you are and how you "should" operate. Some moments may feel significant. Others may seem ordinary. Each one contributes to the framework through which you interpret your life today.

As you move through this week, allow your memories to surface at their own pace. Notice how meaning is attached to certain experiences. Pay attention to what feels charged, familiar, or defining. These signals help illuminate how your identity has been constructed.

This week lays the foundation for the journey ahead. Understanding where your story began creates clarity about what you are carrying forward, and what you may be ready to reshape.

EXERCISE 1: Ambition Timeline

This exercise helps you trace how your understanding of success, worth, and responsibility developed over time. Seeing these moments laid out reveals patterns that often go unquestioned. Move slowly and allow memory and meaning to surface together.

Draw a horizontal line. Mark 5–7 moments that shaped your understanding of:

- ***success***
- ***ambition***
- ***worth***
- ***identity***
- ***strength***
- ***responsibility***

For each point, journal about:
- What happened?
- What did it teach me?
- How do I carry that lesson today?

EXERCISE 2: Identity Origins, Reflection

This exercise invites you to name the roles and identities you learned in order to feel safe, respected, or loved. There is no need to soften or correct your answers. Let honesty lead.

Complete the following sentences:

- *I learned I needed to be _____ to stay safe.*
- *I learned I needed to be _____ to be respected.*
- *I learned I needed to be _____ to be loved.*

Finish this statement:

My early environment taught me to hide or silence...
_____
_____
_____

Week 1 Notes:

WEEK 2: Intergenerational Mapping

Identity does not begin with one generation. Families pass down more than names and traditions. *They pass down emotional patterns, beliefs about safety, interpretations of strength, and strategies for navigating the world.*

This week focuses on your *emotional inheritance*. Many of the ways you respond to stress, responsibility, and connection were modeled long before you had language for them. These patterns often emerge as habits rather than conscious choices.

Intergenerational mapping helps you recognize how family roles, expectations, and survival strategies influenced your development. *Some of these patterns offer resilience, wisdom, and resourcefulness. Others place pressure on the nervous system or limit your emotional expression.*

This work invites you to look at your lineage with clarity and care. You are not assessing or assigning fault. You are noticing how adaptation traveled through generations, and how those adaptations live in you right now.

As you reflect, observe which patterns feel familiar in your body and relationships. Notice which roles you stepped into early, and which responsibilities you learned to carry that weren't yours to begin with. Awareness creates the space to understand what you inherited, and how it shaped you.

Seeing inherited patterns clearly prepares you to decide what you wish to carry forward, and how you want to shape the future that comes through you.

EXERCISE 1: Emotional Lineage Map

This exercise helps you observe emotional patterns across generations without blame or idealization. You are mapping, not diagnosing. Approach this with compassion for both yourself and those who came before you.

Create your 3-generation map:

You → Parents → Grandparents

For each branch, note:

- *Their survival strategies*
- *Emotional expression norms*
- *Spoken/unspoken rules*
- *Strengths they modeled*
- *Wounds they carried*
- *Cultural messages about success, rest, community, and ambition*

EXERCISE 2: Cycle-Breaking Reflection

This exercise supports awareness of how inherited patterns show up in your present-day responses. Notice what feels familiar in your body as you write. Awareness is the first step toward interrupting the cycle.

Step 1: Identify Triggers

- *When my pace speeds up, it's usually because…*
- *I ignore my needs when I feel…*
- *My body signals stress by…*
- *A situation that always pulls me into urgency is…*

Step 2: Patterns to Notice

Check all patterns you experience:

- ☐ *Emotional numbing*
- ☐ *Overworking*
- ☐ *Hyper-independence*
- ☐ *People-pleasing*
- ☐ *Avoidance*
- ☐ *Overresponsibility*
- ☐ *Difficulty receiving support*

Step 3: Reclaim Direction

- *I'm ready to interrupt the pattern of…*
- *I want ambition to feel like…*
- *I will stop draining myself by…*
- *I will protect my energy by…*

Reflections:

_____

_____

Week 2 Notes:

WEEK 3: Unlearning Survival Scripts

Internal Boundaries, Deconditioning & Identity Reclamation

Survival scripts are learned responses that once helped you navigate specific environments. They shape how you relate to work, relationships, rest, and self-expectation. Over time, these scripts can feel indistinguishable from your true identity.

This week centers on recognizing internalized beliefs that influence behavior and decision-making. Many of these beliefs were reinforced through family systems, cultural narratives, gender roles, religious teachings, or social conditioning.

Unlearning is an act of awareness. It involves noticing which beliefs continue to guide you and how they affect your energy, boundaries, and sense of self. Some beliefs may feel deeply aligned. Others may feel restrictive or outdated.

This work invites you to observe your internal landscape with honesty. As beliefs surface, notice how they show up in your body and your emotional responses. These observations provide insight into what is shaping your daily experience.

Internal boundaries begin with truth. Naming what no longer serves your well-being creates room for beliefs that support alignment and intentional choices. This week helps you articulate what you are ready to release, and what you want to reinforce.

Through this process, identity becomes less reactive and more intentional. Awareness opens space for conscious choices and clarity.

EXERCISE 1: Cultural Ambition Belief Audit

This exercise brings long-held beliefs about success, rest, and worth into conscious review. Some may feel protective; others may feel restrictive. You are not required to change anything yet—only to see clearly.

Complete the following sentence:

- *In my family/community, success meant...*
- *Rest was described as...*
- *People who slowed down were...*
- *My worth was tied to...*

Now, label each belief (keep, evolve, or release) with how you want to proceed:

KEEP | EVOLVE | RELEASE

Reflections:

_____
_____
_____
_____
_____
_____

EXERCISE 2: Rewrite One Belief

This exercise invites you to practice choice. Rewriting a belief is not about forcing optimism; it's about aligning language with who you are becoming.

Old belief: _____
New aligned belief: _____

EXERCISE 3: Internal Boundaries Declaration

This exercise helps you articulate the internal agreements that guide how you treat yourself. Write from a place of clarity and self-respect. Boundaries clarify what you will protect, and what you will no longer carry.

- *I am no longer available for…*
- *I release the expectation that I must…*
- *I protect my energy by…*
- *I honor myself by saying no to…*

Reflections:

_____
_____
_____
_____
_____
_____

Week 3 Notes:

WEEK 4: Returning to Values

Values-Based Living, Identity Integration & Alignment

Values serve as internal guides. They shape how (and what) you prioritize, make decisions, and relate to yourself and others. When values are clear and lived out, they bring a sense of direction and coherence. When they are unexamined or inherited without reflection, they can create internal strain.

This week centers on reclaiming values as chosen principles rather than inherited expectations. Many people practice values shaped by family, culture, or survival without realizing it. These values may have been necessary at one point in life, and less supportive now.

Values work invites discernment. It asks you to consider what matters most to you in this season, and how those values are expressed in your daily life. This includes how you use time, energy, and attention.

As you explore your values, notice where alignment feels natural and where tension arises. These moments offer insight into how identity, belief, and behavior intersect. Values clarify what feels meaningful and what feels unsustainable.

This week helps you articulate a values framework that reflects who you are becoming. From this foundation, boundaries strengthen, decisions gain clarity, and self-trust begins to deepen.

Values offer orientation for the work ahead. They become reference points as you move into body awareness, energy protection, reconnection, rhythm, and choice.

EXERCISE 1: Root Values Identification

Read each value description and circle any that resonate in your body (not just your mind).

Integrity — Wholeness in action; alignment between what you say, believe, and do.
Freedom — The ability to choose your actions, rhythms, and identity without pressure or fear.
Generosity — Offering care or presence from fullness, not obligation.
Connection — Being known, seen, understood, and emotionally held.
Spirituality — Honoring the sacred; relationship to faith, nature, ritual, or ancestors.
Growth — Choosing evolution over stagnation, even when uncomfortable.
Legacy — Creating impact that nourishes future generations.
Justice — Alignment with truth, equity, and accountability.
Rest — Restoration as a right, not a reward; nervous system peace.
Creativity — Allowing imagination, art, or innovation to flow freely.
Community — Belonging, reciprocity, shared care.
Truth — Honest communication with yourself and others.
Courage — Acting from alignment even when afraid.
Safety — Emotional and physical environments where you can be whole.
Belonging — Acceptance without fragmentation or performance.
Wisdom — Discernment through lived experience + ancestral knowing.
Transparency — Clarity in intent, communication, and impact.
Harmony — Balance within self, relationships, and environments.
Joy — Fullness, delight, and pleasure as birthright.
Love — Care, commitment, compassion as ongoing practice.
Accountability — Owning impact, repairing harm, honoring commitments.
Ritual — Intentional practices that tether you to self, culture, and spirit.
Trust — Confidence in yourself, others, and the unfolding of life.
Sovereignty — Leading yourself from within; agency, autonomy, boundary-protected identity.

Now, choose 10 values that resonate. Then narrow to 5 core values — the ones that feel non-negotiable.

EXERCISE 2: Values Alignment Reflection

This exercise invites you to observe how your chosen values are currently expressed in your life. *Notice where they are supported, where they feel strained, and where they ask for more care and awareness.*

For each of your 5 values, answer:

1. How is this value showing up in my life right now?
2. Where am I compromising or abandoning this value? Why?
3. What relationships, environments, or beliefs support this value?
4. What pulls me away from living this value?
5. What small, repeatable practice would bring me closer to embodying it?

Reflections:

_____
_____
_____
_____
_____
_____
_____
_____
_____
_____
_____
_____
_____
_____

EXERCISE 3: Values Conflict Audit

This exercise brings attention to moments where important values might pull you in different directions. *These moments offer insight into opportunities for discernment and growth. Stay present with what emerges.*

Identify one area where two of your values conflict (e.g., *Freedom vs. Stability, Rest vs. Responsibility*).

- What's the tension?
- Where did the tension originate?
- Which value aligns with your future self?
- What boundary or decision will honor that?

Reflections:

_____
_____
_____
_____
_____
_____
_____
_____
_____
_____
_____
_____
_____
_____
_____

EXERCISE 4: Values Embodiment Commitment

This exercise turns values into lived practice. *Choose commitments that feel sustainable and supportive. Let consistency shape your progress.*

Complete the following sentences:

- The value I will embody more consciously this month is:
  _____

- I will embody it through:
  _____

- I will protect it by:
  _____

- I will honor it even when challenged by:
  _____

With your values reclaimed, you're ready to listen more deeply to the place where your truth first appears — your body.

Week 4 Notes:

WEEK 5: Body Awareness & Nervous System Literacy

Listening to Internal Signals

The body carries information that often precedes conscious thought. Sensations, tension, ease, and fatigue offer insight into your emotional state, stress levels, and capacity. Many people learn to override these signals in order to meet expectations or maintain performance.

This week centers on rebuilding awareness of bodily cues. Body awareness supports clarity by bringing attention to how your experiences are registered internally. These signals reflect your needs, boundaries, and responses to the environment.

Nervous system literacy helps you recognize patterns of activation and groundedness. Over time, these patterns influence your mood, your focus, and your energy. Learning to notice them supports earlier awareness and more responsive care.

As you move through this week, allow yourself to observe your internal signals without interpretation, and without judgment. Notice sensations as they arise. Pay attention to moments of tension, calmness, or relief. These observations build familiarity with your internal landscape.

This work strengthens self-attunement. Attunement supports the work of discernment by preparing you to manage your energy with greater intention. Listening to your body creates a foundation for sustainable engagement with life.

EXERCISE 1: Body Cues Journal (5–7 Days)

This exercise supports a steady relationship with your body through attention and listening. *Notice patterns as they appear. Return to the practice as needed.*

Use this table to track the following:

Time	Body Cue	Context

Reflection:

- Which cues appeared most frequently?
- Which showed up in moments of ease?
- Which signaled stress or misalignment?

EXERCISE 2: Nervous System Snapshot

This exercise helps you name how your body responds to safety, stress, and grounding. Write what you notice, let the information surface organically.

Complete the following:

- My body speeds up when...
- My body shuts down when...
- I feel grounded when...
- I feel unsafe when...

Reflections:

_____
_____
_____
_____
_____
_____
_____
_____
_____
_____
_____
_____
_____
_____
_____
_____

EXERCISE 3: Survival-to-Safety Scale

This exercise helps you build awareness of how your nervous system moves throughout the day. Your internal state is not fixed; it shifts in response to environment, stress, connection, rest, and self-talk. Learning to notice these shifts strengthens your capacity to respond with care, rather than urgency.

Use this scale as a gentle daily check-in. There is no ideal number. The goal is familiarity with your patterns and an increased ability to recognize what supports grounding.

Survival-to-Safety Scale
Circle the number that best reflects your current state:

1–3 | Survival Mode
You may feel tense, rushed, numb, or emotionally guarded. Your body is focused on getting through.

4–6 | Transition
You may feel mixed or unsettled, moving between tension and calm. Your body is beginning to soften or stabilize.

7–10 | Grounded
You may feel present, steady, and connected to yourself. Your body experiences a sense of safety or ease.

Daily Reflection:

- What helped me shift upward today, even slightly?
- What pulled me downward or increased tension?
- What did my body need in that moment?

Week 5 Notes:

WEEK 6: Energy Boundaries & Capacity Protection

Stewarding Your Energy

Your energy shapes how you show up in every aspect of your life. It influences your attention, emotional availability, and decision-making. Energy is affected by responsibilities, environments, relationships, and internal expectations. Without self-awareness, your energy is often depleted before it is protected.

This week centers on understanding your capacity and stewardship. Capacity includes physical stamina, emotional availability, and mental focus. Recognizing your capacity helps you respond to demands with clarity rather than urgency.

Energetic boundaries define what you are available for and how you engage. These boundaries support you by clarifying your limits and your priorities. They allow you to allocate your energy in ways that align with your values and needs.

As you explore your energetic patterns, notice where your energy feels sustained and where it feels diminished. Pay attention to early signals of strain or overload. These signals offer guidance about ways to adjust and manage self-care.

This week supports intentional engagement. Protecting your capacity allows you to move through life with greater presence and aligned choices. Energy stewardship prepares you for deeper reconnection, rhythm-building, and values-based decision-making in the weeks ahead.

EXERCISE 1: Energy Budget

This exercise helps you understand how your energy is currently being allocated across your life. *Energy is shaped by habits, expectations, and environments long before it becomes exhaustion. Seeing it clearly allows you to make choices with intention instead of reaction.*

Begin by listing what consistently fuels you and what consistently drains you. Notice patterns rather than isolated moments. Some drains may be necessary; others may be adjustable. Awareness gives you leverage.

Energy Budget:

- Inputs (what sustains or restores me):
_____
_____

- Outputs (what consistently drains me):
_____
_____

Alignment Reflection:

- Which drains feel unavoidable right now?
- Which drains could be reduced, delegated, or bounded?
- What input feels most essential to protect?

EXERCISE 2: The Capacity Boundary Line

This exercise helps you become fluent in your personal signals of capacity. *Capacity is not only about time or energy; it includes emotional availability, cognitive load, and nervous system regulation.* When you can recognize your internal thresholds early, you are better able to make decisions that protect sustainability.

Begin by reflecting on each state as it shows up *in your body, your emotions, and your behavior.* Be specific. Your cues are unique.

Below Capacity

When I am below capacity, I notice:

- In my body:
  _____

- In my emotions:
  _____

- In my behavior or communication:
  _____

At Capacity

When I am at capacity, I notice:

- In my body:
  _____

- In my emotions:
  _____

- In my behavior or communication:
  _____

Over Capacity

When I am over capacity, I notice:

- In my body:
  _____

- In my emotions:
  _____

- In my behavior or communication:
  _____

Reflection:

- Which state do I habitually operate in?
- What typically pushes me past my capacity line?
- What early signal tells me I am approaching my limit?
- What is one adjustment that will help me stay within my capacity more consistently?

EXERCISE 3: Energetic Realignment

This exercise helps you translate awareness into action. Once you understand your capacity and energy patterns, realignment happens through small, intentional choices that protect your nervous system and reinforce self-trust. *Realignment is not about correcting yourself; it is about choosing differently with clarity.*

Focus on what will *meaningfully* support you this week. Choose actions that are realistic within your current responsibilities and energy.

Boundary to Hold:

1. A boundary I will hold this week is:

_____

2. This boundary supports my energy by:

_____

3. I will know I am honoring this boundary when:

_____

Energy Input to Commit To:

1. One energy input I will commit to this week is:

_____

2. This input supports me by:

_____

3. I will protect this input by:

_____

Weekly Check-In
At the end of the week, reflect briefly:

- How did holding this boundary affect my energy or mood?
- What shifted when I protected this input?

Gentle reminder: Alignment strengthens through repeated, intentional choices.

Week 6 Notes:

WEEK 7: Returning to the Self

Reclaiming the Parts You Silenced

Identity is not fixed. It unfolds, adapts, and reshapes itself across the seasons of your life. *As you move through different environments, roles, and responsibilities, certain parts of you become more visible while others recede into the background.* These shifts often occur without conscious choice, shaped by what is required of you to belong, to succeed, or to remain steady.

Many people lose regular access to parts of themselves that once felt natural and alive:

- the playful part
- the creative part
- the intuitive part
- the rested part
- the expressive part
- the courageous part

Over time, responsibility, expectations, performance, and *survival demands* influence which parts of the self are welcomed forward and which are asked to stay quiet. Certain qualities receive reinforcement because they help you navigate the world effectively. Others receive less space, less attention, or less permission to exist openly.

These adaptations often serve a purpose. They help maintain safety, stability, and belonging within specific contexts. *Family dynamics, cultural messages, educational environments, workplaces, and relational expectations all shape how identity is expressed.* In many cases, composure, resilience, and contribution become central, while softness, rest, creativity, or emotional expression are placed on hold.

This week is an emotional homecoming. It centers on recognizing the parts of yourself that have been quieted, deprioritized, or set aside over time. Some of these parts may feel distant. Others may feel tender or immediately familiar. Each response offers insight into how your identity has been shaped and protected.

Returning to self begins with naming:

- the parts of you that faded into the background
- the qualities that received less space or care
- the expressions of self that still seek acknowledgment

Naming brings awareness. Awareness creates space. As you move through this week, allow yourself to notice what feels tender, familiar, or quietly energizing. These sensations offer information about what is ready to return into right relationship with you.

Reconnection unfolds through presence. It does not require urgency or force. It develops as you acknowledge what has been waiting for your attention and allow it to be seen, without pressure to perform.

This work supports wholeness. Wholeness creates coherence. Coherence becomes the ground from which a sustainable legacy is lived. *As you engage this week, let curiosity guide you. Let recognition lead. This is an invitation to come home to yourself, one part at a time.*

EXERCISE 1: The Self-Return Map

This exercise supports reconnection with parts of yourself that may have been quieted over time in response to responsibility, expectation, or survival. These parts were not lost; they adapted. Returning to them happens through recognition, care, and consistent presence.

Step 1 — What I've Silenced

List up to five parts of yourself that feel distant, muted, or under-expressed.

Examples may include: the playful part, the creative part, the expressive part, the intuitive part, the rested part, the hopeful part.

Parts I've silenced or set aside:

1. _____
2. _____
3. _____
4. _____
5. _____

Step 2 — Glimpses of Return

For each part you named, recall a moment—recent or distant—when you felt connected to it.

As you reflect, notice:

- What was happening around you?
- What did you feel in your body?
- What emotions or sensations were present?

Reflections:

_____

_____

_____

_____

Step 3 — Barriers

This step brings awareness to what makes sustained connection difficult. Common barriers include overworking, fear of judgment, emotional fatigue, internalized expectations, relationship dynamics, or environments that require performance.

Barriers I notice most often:

_____

_____

_____

What these barriers protect me from:

_____

_____

_____

Step 4 — Rituals of Return

Choose one simple, repeatable action to reconnect with each part you named. These rituals do not need to be elaborate. They need to be consistent and supportive.

For each part:

- What helps it feel safe to re-emerge?
- What environment or boundary supports it?

_____

_____

_____

_____

Week 7 Notes:

WEEK 8: Rituals, Rhythms & Sustainability

Consistency That Holds Alignment

As parts of yourself begin to return, they require care and continuity. Awareness deepens when it is revisited, intentionally. Insight settles when it is given rhythm. *Without regular points of return, even meaningful realizations can fade beneath the pace of daily life.*

This week centers on rhythm as a stabilizing force. Rhythms create predictable moments of connection. They offer your body, mind, and nervous system repeated opportunities to orient toward steadiness, reflection, and presence. Over time, these moments shape how alignment is experienced and sustained.

Many people associate change with intensity or motivation. What supports sustainability is continuity. Rhythms help carry you through periods of energy, fatigue, clarity, and uncertainty. They provide structure that does not rely on willpower or urgency.

Rituals are intentional rhythms. They mark time, anchor your values, and create space for self-care. A ritual can be quiet or simple, and its meaning comes from repetition and *intention*. When rituals align with your real life, they become reliable points of grounding.

This week invites you to notice:

- how you currently move through your days and weeks
- where reflection or self-care already exists
- where continuity would support greater steadiness

As you design rhythms, be sure to assess how well they fit in your day-to-day. Consider what your body responds to, what your energy can hold, and what your current season allows. *Sustainable rhythms* support presence without requiring constant adjustment.

Rituals also reinforce relationship with the self. Returning to the same practice, the same moment, or the same moments of pause, builds familiarity and trust. Over time, these returns shape how you listen inward and respond to your needs.

The work of this week is not about creating an ideal schedule. It is about establishing patterns that make your inner alignment accessible. As you move through the exercises, let your rhythms reflect care, intention, and continuity. These rhythms will carry forward into decision-making, purpose, and legacy.

EXERCISE 1: Weekly Alignment Ritual

This exercise establishes a steady rhythm for reflection and recalibration. Alignment is sustained through regular attention to values, energy, and lived experience. A weekly ritual creates continuity and supports integration over time.

Choose one consistent moment each week to return to this practice. Let your reflections unfold without urgency. This is a space for listening and noticing.

Weekly Reflection

As you reflect on the past week, consider the following:

- Where did I experience clarity, steadiness, or ease?
- Where did I notice tension, fatigue, or emotional weight?
- What signals did my body communicate most clearly?
- Which moments felt nourishing or supportive?
- What patterns became visible as I looked back over the week?

Take your time. Allow your responses to reflect both what you noticed and what you felt.

As you move into the coming week, identify one small adjustment that supports alignment:

1. One adjustment I will carry forward is:

_____

2. How this adjustment supports my values or capacity:

_____

3. What will help me remember to return to this practice:

_____

EXERCISE 2: Ritual Design

This exercise supports the creation of rhythms that sustain alignment over time. Rituals provide structure for care, reflection, and grounding. They help translate values into lived experience by offering predictable moments of return.

Rituals do not need to be elaborate or time-intensive. Their power comes from consistency, intention, and meaning. This exercise invites you to design rituals that fit your real life and support your capacity.

Identifying Supportive Rituals

Begin by choosing two rituals—daily or weekly—that feel accessible and nourishing in this season of your life.

As you choose, consider:

- What helps me feel connected to myself?
- What supports steadiness in my body or emotions?
- What rhythms feel sustainable right now?

Ritual 1

Name of ritual: _____

1. When this ritual will occur (time/day):

_____

2. What this ritual supports in me (energy, clarity, grounding, connection):

_____

3. What helps me stay consistent with this ritual:

_____

_____

Ritual 2

Name of ritual: _____

1. When this ritual will occur (time/day):

_____

2. What this ritual supports in me (energy, clarity, grounding, connection):

_____

3. What helps me stay consistent with this ritual:

_____

_____

Reflection:

As you consider these rituals, reflect briefly:

- How do these rituals support the person I am becoming?
- What environments, boundaries, or reminders help these rituals remain present in my life?

Week 8 Notes:

WEEK 9: Values-Based Decision Making & Self-Trust

Choosing from Internal Alignment

As reconnection with yourself deepens and rhythm becomes established, clarity begins to take shape. This clarity influences how decisions are experienced and made. Choices start to reflect your values, capacity, and internal coherence rather than momentum alone.

Decision-making is an ongoing practice. Every choice carries information about what you are prioritizing, protecting, and cultivating. Over time, patterns of decision-making shape your relationship with yourself. They influence self-trust, direction, and how grounded you feel in your life.

Values play a central role in this process. They inform what feels meaningful, what feels misaligned, and what feels sustainable. When your values are attended to regularly, they offer guidance during moments of uncertainty, pressure, or transition.

Self-trust develops through repeated experiences of listening inward and responding with intention. It strengthens as you notice how decisions feel in your body and emotions. Clarity often shows up as steadiness, presence, or a sense of internal agreement. *These signals offer guidance about alignment.*

This week centers on discernment. Discernment grows through awareness, reflection, and alignment. It is shaped by your values, supported by your rhythms, and informed by your capacity. As these elements come together, decision-making becomes more embodied and intentional.

During this week, allow yourself to focus on how your choices are formed and felt. Pay attention to moments when decisions carry a sense of direction or ease. These experiences reveal how alignment shows up for you and how self-trust is practiced over time.

Choice becomes a form of self-leadership when it reflects clarity, care, and continuity. *This week supports your ability to choose in ways that honor who you are becoming, and the life you are shaping.* From this foundation, purpose, vision, and legacy begin to take clearer form.

EXERCISE 1: Values Alignment Test

This exercise supports clarity in how decisions are made and felt. Every choice carries information about values, capacity, and self-trust. *When decisions align internally, they tend to feel settled and coherent in the body.*

Choose one recent decision—small or significant—to reflect on. Let your attention rest on your experience rather than the outcome.

Decision Reflection

1. The decision I am reflecting on is:

_____

2. Values present in this decision:

_____

3. Values that felt strained or unexpressed:

_____

4. Sensations or signals I noticed in my body while making this decision:

_____

5. What this decision revealed about my current priorities:

_____

_____

Reflection:

Based on this reflection, one insight I want to carry forward into future decisions is:

_____

EXERCISE 2: The Aligned Yes / The Aligned No

This exercise strengthens discernment by clarifying what you are available for and what you are not. Alignment becomes tangible through intentional "yeses" and thoughtful boundaries. Over time, these choices build trust with yourself.

The Aligned Yes

1. One commitment, invitation, or direction I am choosing to say yes to is:

_____

2. This yes supports my values by:

_____

3. I will know this yes remains aligned when I notice:

_____

_____

The Aligned No

1. One request, pattern, or expectation I am choosing to release is:

_____

2. Releasing this supports my capacity by:

_____

3. I will reinforce this no by:

_____

_____

Closing Reflection:

As I practice aligned yeses and nos, I notice the following shifts in my energy, clarity, or self-trust:_____

Week 9 Notes:

WEEK 10: Purpose, Vision & Legacy Orientation

Designing the Life You Are Meant to Live

As awareness deepens and decision-making becomes more intentional, a larger question begins to surface: *What am I orienting my life toward?* This week centers on purpose and vision as *lived direction* rather than abstract aspiration.

Purpose is not a role or title. It reflects how you move through your life, what you prioritize, and the meaning you assign to your efforts. Vision offers perspective. It helps you see beyond immediate demands and situate your choices within a longer horizon.

Many people pursue goals without examining the internal environment those goals create. This week invites you to consider the emotional, relational, and energetic qualities you want your life to hold. Vision becomes clearer when it reflects not only what you want to build, but how you want to experience your days.

This work supports *intentional design*. It asks you to imagine your life as something shaped through values, boundaries, and choice as a response rather than a reaction. Vision at this stage draws on the clarity you've developed about yourself, your energy, and your decision-making.

As you move through this week, focus on your direction rather than your destination. Notice what feels meaningful for you to cultivate within you, and what feels important to protect. Purpose emerges through attention, care, and consistency of choice over time.

This week prepares you to articulate the broader shape of the life you are building and the legacy it will reflect.

EXERCISE 1: Legacy Intention, Part 1

Clarifying the Life You Are Orienting Toward

This exercise helps you articulate the deeper orientation guiding your life right now. Legacy is shaped through what you prioritize, protect, and practice over time. This reflection invites you to name what you are consciously cultivating through your choices.

Take a moment to settle before you begin. Let your responses reflect what feels meaningful in this season rather than what feels impressive or expected.

Legacy Intention Reflection

1. The values that must be present in the life I am building are:

_____

2. The emotional environment I want to experience in my daily life includes:

_____

3. The version of myself I am becoming is characterized by:

_____

4. The people, relationships, or future generations I am considering as I shape my life include:

_____

5. What feels most important for me to honor as I move forward is:

_____

6. When I act in alignment with this intention, I notice:

_____

_____

EXERCISE 2: Embodying Your Vision

Imagining Your Ideal Life

This exercise invites you to imagine your life from the inside out. Vision here is not about prediction or achievement. It is about sensing how your life feels when it reflects your values, priorities, and care for yourself.

Find a quiet moment. Allow images and sensations to arise naturally. Write in the present tense.

Guided Vision Reflection

1. A day in my life feels like:

___

2. My pace throughout the day includes:

___

3. The way I move through my responsibilities feels:

___

4. My relationships feel characterized by:

___

5. My body feels:

___

6. The energy I bring into spaces feels:

___

Closing Reflection:

As I imagine this life, what stands out most is:

___

EXERCISE 3: Alignment Check

Living Out Your Vision

This exercise bridges vision and aligned action. It helps you identify where your current life already reflects your intended direction and where gentle adjustments may be needed.

Review your reflections above, then respond with honesty and care.

Reflection:

Three aspects of my current life that already reflect this vision are:

1. _____
2. _____
3. _____

One area of my life that is asking for clearer direction is:

_____

One small shift that would support this direction is:

_____

What will help me remember this direction during demanding moments is:

_____

_____

Week 10 Notes:

WEEK 11: The Five Pillars of a Sovereign Life

Creating a Foundation That Holds What You Build

A meaningful vision requires support. *Without a strong foundation, even well-defined goals can become unsustainable.* This week introduces the Five Pillars as a framework for supporting the life you are designing.

Each pillar represents a dimension of your lived experience that contributes to long-term well-being and agency:

- **Purpose** — direction and meaning
- **Peace** — internal regulation and emotional safety
- **Partnership** — mutual support and relational nourishment
- **Play** — joy, creativity, and freedom
- **Practice** — habits and rituals that reinforce alignment

This framework helps you assess where your life currently feels supported and where additional care is needed. It offers language for understanding imbalance without judgment, and structure for making thoughtful adjustments when needed.

As you engage this week, consider how these pillars show up in your daily life. Notice which feel well-resourced for you, and which feel under-attended. Each pillar contributes to how sustainable your vision becomes over time.

This work invites you to strengthen the conditions that allow for growth without depletion. A well-supported foundation allows your purpose and vision to unfold with integrity.

The Five Pillars serve as an organizing framework you can return to as life evolves and priorities shift.

EXERCISE 1: Pillar Assessment

Understanding What Is Supporting Your Life Right Now

This exercise helps you take inventory of how the major dimensions of your life are currently supported. Each pillar represents an area that influences how sustainable your life feels in practice. *Move through each pillar slowly. Let your answers reflect what is true in this season of your life.*

1. Purpose
How are direction and meaning currently experienced in my life?

_____

Examples: feeling clear about why you do your work · feeling disconnected from your long-term direction · sensing purpose mainly through responsibility to others

2. Peace
How do I currently experience emotional regulation and internal safety?

_____

Examples: frequent mental noise · moments of calm during specific routines · feeling emotionally guarded in certain environments

3. Partnership
How does support, connection, and reciprocity show up in my relationships?

_____

Examples: being relied on more than supported · having one relationship that feels mutually nourishing · receiving care inconsistently

4. Play
How does joy, creativity, and freedom show up currently in my life?

_____

Examples: joy appearing only during time off · creative expression feeling distant · moments of lightness through hobbies or movement

5. Practice
How do my habits, rituals, or routines support my care and growth?

_____

Examples: inconsistent routines · one grounding practice that feels stabilizing · structure that exists mainly around work demands

EXERCISE 2: Pillar Strengthening

Identifying What Each Pillar Needs

This exercise invites you to identify what would most support each pillar right now. Support may involve adding something, adjusting something, or protecting what already exists.

1. Purpose
One way this pillar could be more supported is:

_____

Examples: clarifying a longer-term direction · reconnecting with why your work matters · redefining success in this season

2. Peace
One way this pillar could be more supported is:

_____

Examples: fewer emotionally demanding commitments · clearer emotional boundaries · regular moments of quiet or decompression

3. Partnership
One way this pillar could be more supported is:

_____

Examples: asking for help more directly · strengthening one reciprocal relationship · reducing over-functioning in certain dynamics

4. Play
One way this pillar could be more supported is:

_____

Examples: scheduling time for creative expression · allowing enjoyment without justification · reintroducing activities that feel enlivening

5. Practice
One way this pillar could be more supported is:

_____

Examples: simplifying routines · choosing one practice to return to consistently · creating structure that supports rest and reflection

EXERCISE 3: Pillar Actions

Translating Structure Into Practice

This exercise turns reflection into action. Choose one small, concrete action for each pillar that feels doable within your current capacity. These actions are meant to be practiced, not perfected.

One Action Per Pillar

1. Purpose —

_____

Examples: journaling weekly about direction · dedicating focused time to meaningful work · revisiting personal goals monthly

2. Peace —

_____

Examples: ending the day without screens · taking intentional pauses during work · limiting emotionally draining conversations

3. Partnership —

_____

Examples: initiating one honest check-in · receiving support without minimizing needs · setting clearer expectations in a key relationship

4. Play —

_____

Examples: engaging in a creative hobby weekly · moving your body for enjoyment · spending unstructured time outdoors

5. Practice —

_____

Examples: morning grounding ritual · evening reflection practice · weekly planning rooted in care rather than urgency

EXERCISE 4: Environmental Support

Ensuring Your Life Can Hold What You Are Building

This exercise helps you consider how your environment influences the pillars you are strengthening. *Environment* includes physical space, schedules, expectations, and relational dynamics.

1. Elements of my environment that currently support these pillars include:

_____

Examples: flexible schedule · quiet physical space · access to supportive people

2. Elements of my environment that place strain on these pillars include:

_____

Examples: constant availability expectations · cluttered spaces · emotionally demanding settings

3. One adjustment that would help my environment better support my life is:

_____

Examples: restructuring a schedule · redefining availability · changing how space is used

Closing Reflection:

As I strengthen these pillars, I notice the following shift in how I experience my life:

_____

_____

Week 11 Notes:

WEEK 12: The Legacy Manifesto & Sustainability Plan

A Life Designed with Intention

This final week centers on articulation and integration. Over the past twelve weeks, you have explored identity, inheritance, values, bodily awareness, energy stewardship, reconnection, rhythm, discernment, and vision. What remains now is to gather what you have clarified into language and structure it in ways that can guide you forward.

Legacy is shaped through lived orientation. It is expressed through how you relate to yourself, how you move through relationships, and how you make choices across time. This week invites you to name that orientation clearly and design the conditions that support it.

The work here is not about summarizing everything you have learned. It is about distilling what matters most and giving it form—so that you can return to it like a compass when life becomes demanding or unclear.

Legacy is shaped through what you consistently embody and reinforce. Your legacy is already in motion.

EXERCISE 1: The Legacy Manifesto

Articulating the Life You Are Committed to Living

This exercise helps you put language to the essence of what you are building and embodying. *A manifesto is a declaration of intention and orientation. It reflects how you choose to live, what you choose to protect, and what you choose to prioritize.*

Write slowly, and let your words reflect your truth. This manifesto is meant to serve as a reference point for future decisions and seasons.

Legacy Manifesto Prompt

Complete the following statement in your own words:

My legacy is to

_____

by

_____

so that

_____

_____

Reflection

As I read this statement, I notice:

_____

The values that feel most present in this manifesto are:

_____

The kind of life this manifesto points toward feels:

_____

EXERCISE 2: The 12-Month Sustainability Plan

Designing Conditions That Support Your Legacy

This exercise grounds your manifesto in lived reality. *Sustainability comes from creating conditions that support what you value over time.* This plan reflects your understanding of yourself, your capacity, and your needs.

Focus on what you can realistically maintain. This plan is meant to support returning to yourself, over and over again.

Sustainability Planning

1. The practices or rituals I will maintain are:

_____

Examples: weekly reflection · morning grounding · protected rest time

2. The boundaries I will honor are:

_____

Examples: limits around availability · boundaries with work demands · emotional boundaries in relationships

3. The relationships, environments, or supports that nourish me include:

_____

Examples: specific people · supportive spaces · professional or community resources

4. The values I am committed to embodying consistently are:

_____

_____

EXERCISE 3: The Return Plan

How You Will Come Back to Yourself

This exercise prepares you for moments of drifting, transition, or pressure. Recalibration is a part of living. *Having a plan supports gentler re-entry into alignment and self-care.*

Return Reflection

1. When I notice I am disconnected, depleted, or misaligned, I will:

_____

2. The signs that tell me I need to return include:

_____

3. The practices or reminders that help me reconnect include:

_____

4. The parts of this workbook I am most likely to revisit are:

_____

Closing Reflection:

As I complete this workbook, the most meaningful shift I notice is:

_____

The way I now relate to myself feels:

_____

Week 12 Notes:

Living Your Legacy: Final Thoughts

What you have clarified here is meant to move with you. The language you've shaped, the reflections you've named, and the structures you've designed are living references. They offer orientation and recalibration during moments of choice, transition, and renewal.

This work was never about arriving at a fixed version of yourself. It was about restoring a relationship with who you are and how you want to live. The practices, plans, and commitments you've created are meant to support discernment, care, and responsiveness as life unfolds.

Legacy takes shape through how you inhabit your days. It is expressed through the boundaries you honor, the values you return to, and the way you treat your inner life with respect. It lives in your presence, your decisions, and your willingness to listen inward.

Throughout these twelve weeks, you have engaged in remembering, releasing, and rebuilding. You have traced your story, examined what you inherited, clarified what matters, listened to your body, protected your energy, reconnected with yourself, and shaped direction with intention. Each of these acts contributes to how your life is held and expressed.

There will be seasons that feel expansive and seasons that feel constricting. In each one, you have a way back. The path forward remains available through return.

Return to your values.
Return to your body.
Return to your truth.
Return to yourself.

This is how legacy is lived.

With care,
Anastacia Sams, MA, LMFT
Founder & CEO, *HealingWorks®*

About the Author

Anastacia Sams, MA, LMFT is the Founder and CEO of *HealingWorks®*, a wellness and leadership development company that supports high-achieving professionals in building lives rooted in clarity, capacity, and sustainable success.

As a licensed marriage and family therapist, leadership coach, and educator, Anastacia's work sits at the intersection of identity, emotional wellness, and legacy. She supports individuals and organizations in understanding how inherited patterns, cultural expectations, and unexamined ambition shape the way we live, lead, and relate—and how intentional design creates lives that feel more meaningful.

Anastacia is the creator of the HealingWorks® Legacy Framework™, a proprietary methodology that integrates values-based living, emotional literacy, and embodied self-leadership. Her work is known for its depth, precision, and cultural grounding, offering structure that supports reflection, discernment, and long-term care.

Through HealingWorks®, Anastacia facilitates transformative experiences across coaching, education, and enterprise wellness, helping people reconnect with themselves and shape legacies grounded in presence, intention, and integrity.

www.ingramcontent.com/pod-product-compliance
Lightning Source LLC
LaVergne TN
LVHW081458060526
838201LV00057BA/3067